COLOUR YOUR WAY TO BETTER FOCUS

ART FOR MINDFULNESS
GEOMETRICS

PATTERNS BY ANDY PACIOREK

D1335705

Harper Thorsons
An imprint of HarperCollins*Publishers*
1 London Bridge Street
London SE1 9GF
www.harpercollins.co.uk

First published by HarperCollins*Publishers* in 2015
1 3 5 7 9 10 8 6 4 2

Copyright © 2015 HarperCollins*Publishers*

Patterns by Andy Paciorek
Introduction text by Imi Lo

A catalogue record for this book is available from the British Library

ISBN 978-0-00-794751-5

Printed and bound in China

Introduction

Mindfulness has become extremely popular in recent years, as scientists discover more about the wide array of benefits it has to offer—reducing stress, increasing joy, enhancing emotional intelligence, and undoing bad habits. Although it can be defined in various ways, mindfulness is most simply described as approaching the present moment non-judgementally, and with curiosity. It offers a break from our incessant, autopilot mind, and provides the opportunity to live a fuller life.

Despite urban myth, mindfulness practise is not simply about sitting uncomfortably, or chanting "Omm". *Art for Mindfulness* lies in the intersection of mindfulness and therapeutic art, offering a doorway into mindfulness that is accessible, relatable, and fun. Feeling burdened by the chaos of modern life, many adults have found that colouring helps them reconnect with a simpler, more spontaneous way of being.

In order to reap the most benefits from this book, I would invite you to approach it with a playful and curious attitude. A few partially coloured-in patterns follow for use as inspiration before you embark on your own work. However, despite what your art teacher may have told you in school, there is absolutely no right or wrong way of colouring. You may be pleasantly surprised by the outcome when you trust your instinct and allow colour and strokes to naturally unfold; you may discover a deep sense of calm when you begin to pay the activity your full attention. You may also find this to be a great way to develop more soulful connections with those around you. I hope that you not only enjoy this book, but also discover a deeper layer of spiritual practise through immersing in the art of mindful colouring.

Imi Lo (UKCP, HCPC, MMH), Art Psychotherapist and Mindfulness Teacher

"If the doors of perception were cleansed, everything would appear to man as it is, infinite."

William Blake

"Be happy in the moment; that's enough. Each moment is all we need, not more."

Mother Teresa

"No problem is ever solved in the same consciousness that was used to create it."

Albert Einstein

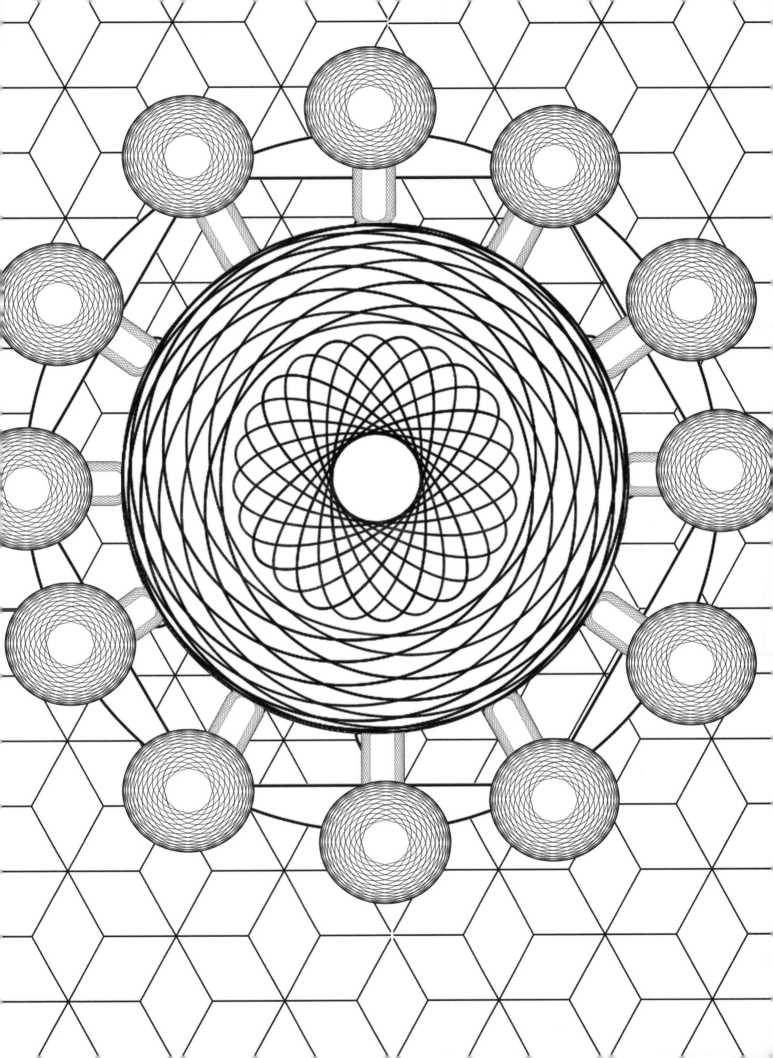

"When you make friends with the present moment, you feel at home no matter where you are."

Eckhart Tolle

"Smile, breathe, and go slowly."

Thích Nhất Hạnh

"We rarely hear the inward music,
but we're dancing to it nevertheless."

Rumi

"He who knows others is wise; he who knows himself is enlightened."

Lao-Tzu

"This is the real secret of life—
to be completely engaged with
what you are doing in the
here and now. And instead of
calling it work, realize it is play."

Alan W. Watts

"Each morning we are born again. What we do today is what matters most."

Buddha

"In the dew of little things, the heart finds its morning and is refreshed."

Kahlil Gibran

"Imagination needs 'moodling'— long, inefficient, happy idling, dawdling, and puttering."

Brenda Ueland

"The meeting of two eternities, the past and future . . . is precisely the present moment."

Henry David Thoreau

"If you want the truth, I'll tell you the truth: Listen to the secret sound, the real sound, which is inside you."

Kabir

"I wanted to change the world. But I have found that the only thing one can be sure of changing is oneself."

Aldous Huxley

**"We never obtain peace
in the outer world
until we make peace
with ourselves."**

The Dalai Lama

"Be quite still and solitary.
The world will freely offer itself to you
to be unmasked. It has no choice.
It will roll in ecstasy at your feet."

Franz Kafka

**"Your vision will become clear
only when you look into your heart.
Who looks outside, dreams.
Who looks inside, awakens."**

Carl Jung

"Paradise is not a place; it is a state of consciousness."

Sri Chinmoy

**"Don't believe everything you think.
Thoughts are just that—thoughts."**

Allan Lokos

"Life is a process of becoming,
a combination of states we have to
go through. Where people fail is that
they wish to elect a state and remain
in it. This is a kind of death."

Anaïs Nin

"Each time for the first time. Each moment the only moment."

Jon Kabat-Zinn

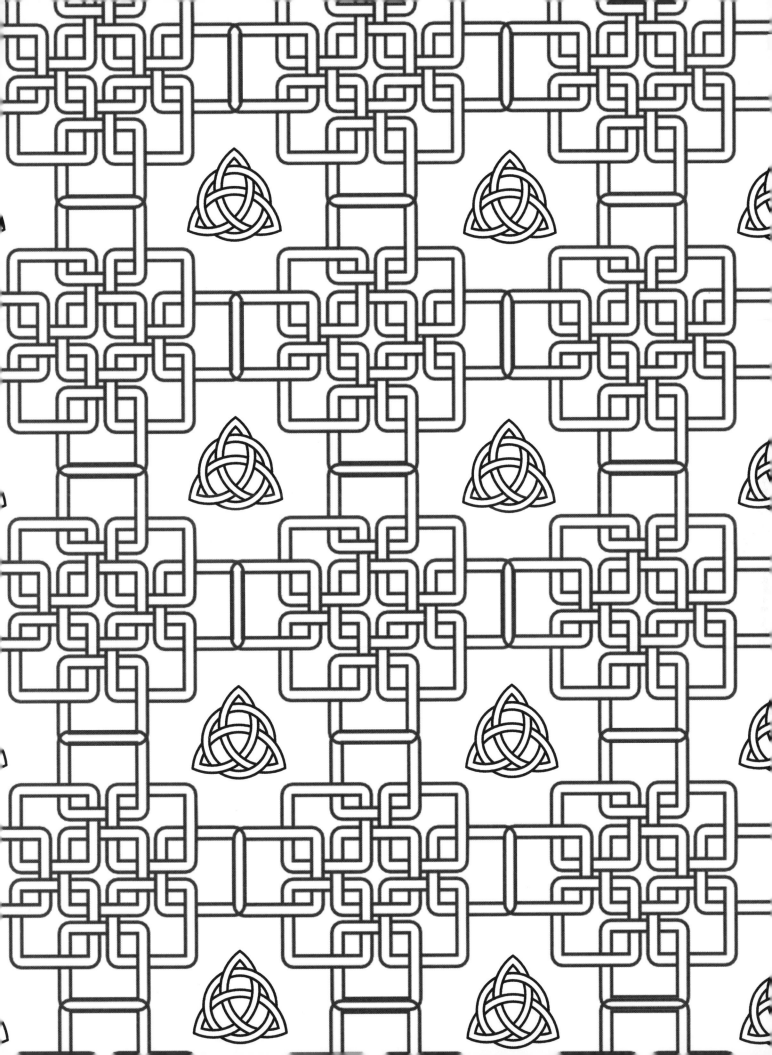

"A mind too active is no mind at all."

Theodore Roethke

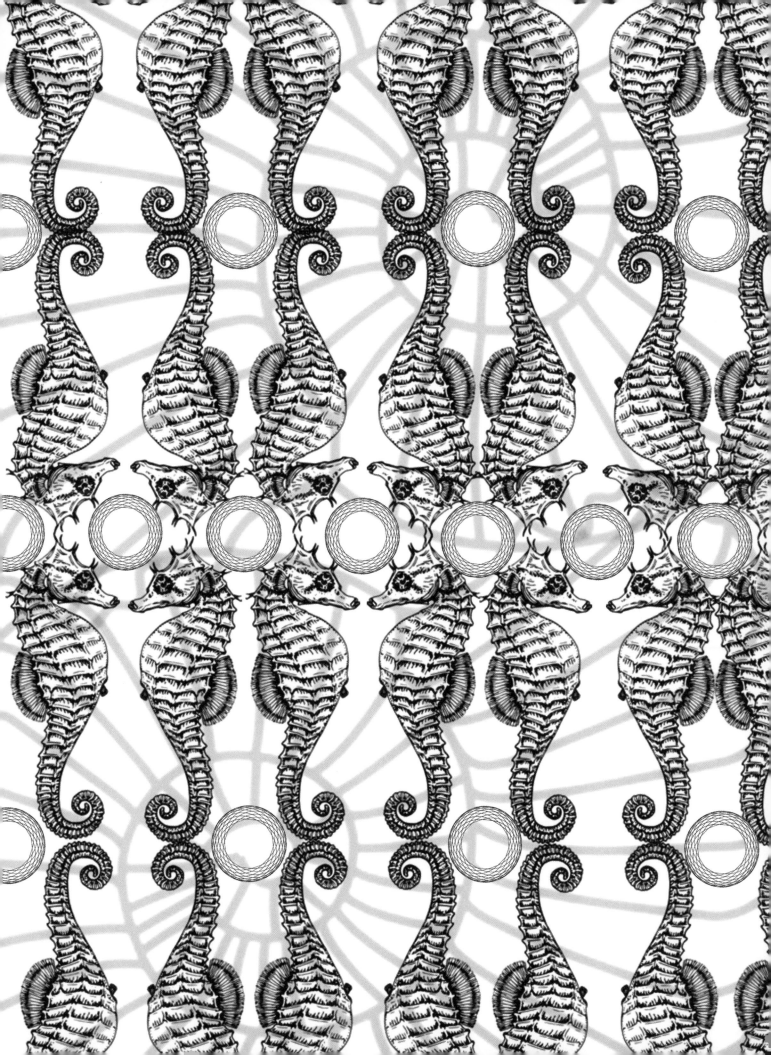

"It's only when we truly know and understand that we have a limited time on earth—and that we have no way of knowing when our time is up—that we will begin to live each day to the fullest, as if it was the only one we had."

Elisabeth Kübler-Ross

"We are what we repeatedly do. Excellence, then, is not an act, but a habit."

Aristotle

"Go into yourself and see how deep the place is from which your life flows."

Rainer Maria Rilke

"The past exists only in our memories, the future only in our plans. The present is our only reality."

Robert M. Pirsig

"In mindfulness, acceptance always comes first; change comes after."

Shamash Alidina

"To understand the immeasurable, the mind must be extraordinarily quiet, still."

Jiddu Krishnamurti

"The most potent muse of all is our own inner child."

Stephen Nachmanovitch

"Every moment is utterly unique and will not be continued in eternity. This fact gives life its poignancy and should concentrate your attention on what you are experiencing now."

Joseph Campbell

"Develop an interest in life as you see it: the people, things, literature, music—the world is so rich, simply throbbing with rich treasures, beautiful souls, and interesting people. Forget yourself."

Henry Miller

"The passing moment is all that we can be sure of; it is only common sense to extract its utmost value from it."

W. Somerset Maugham

"World peace must develop from inner peace. Peace is not just mere absence of violence. Peace is, I think, the manifestation of human compassion."

The Dalai Lama

"Breathe out, look in, let go."

John Welwood

**"You think you understand one.
You think you understand two,
because one and one make two.
But, you must also understand 'and'."**

Sufi proverb

Stop. Breathe. Repeat.

"Silence is the great teacher and to learn its lessons you must pay attention to it. There is no substitute for the creative inspiration, knowledge, and stability that come from knowing how to contact your core of inner silence."

Deepak Chopra

"A discovery is said to be an accident meeting a prepared mind."

Albert Szent-Gyorgyi

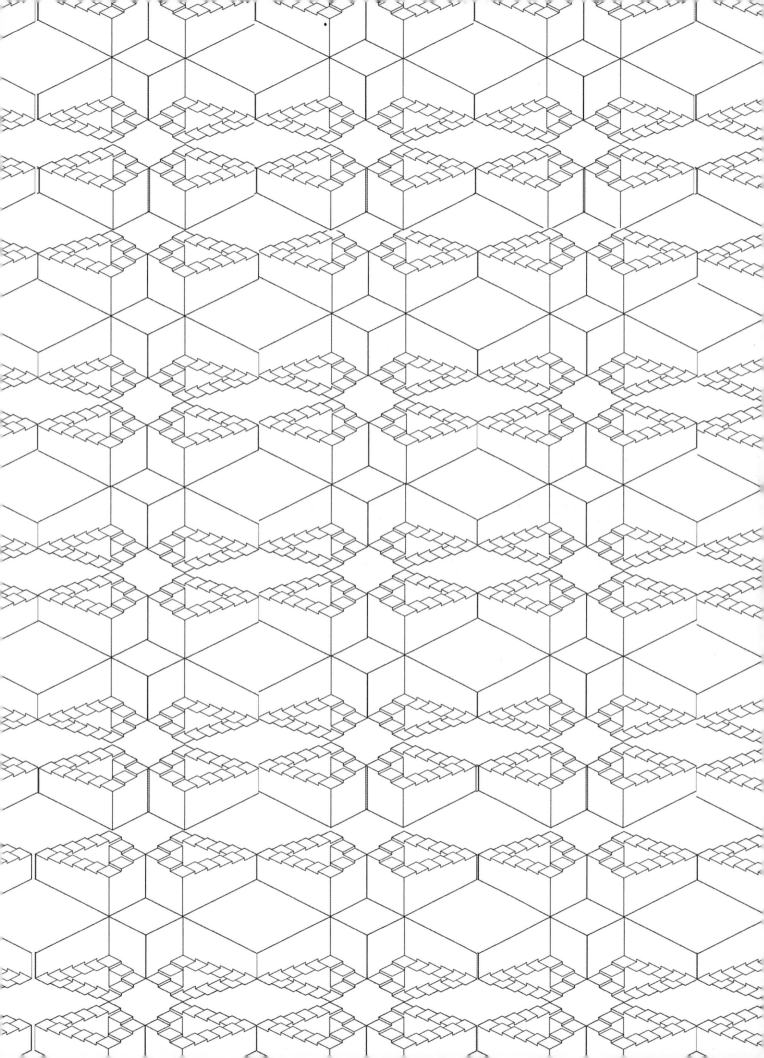

"Restore your attention or bring it to a new level by dramatically slowing down whatever you're doing."

Sharon Salzberg

"He who knows all the answers has not been asked all the questions."

Confucius

"The place to be happy is here.
The time to be happy is now."

Robert G. Ingersoll

"There is something in every one of you that waits and listens for the sound of the genuine in yourself. It is the only true guide you will ever have."

Howard Thurman

"Let go of your mind and then be mindful. Close your ears and listen."

Rumi

"The only journey is the journey within."

Rainer Maria Rilke

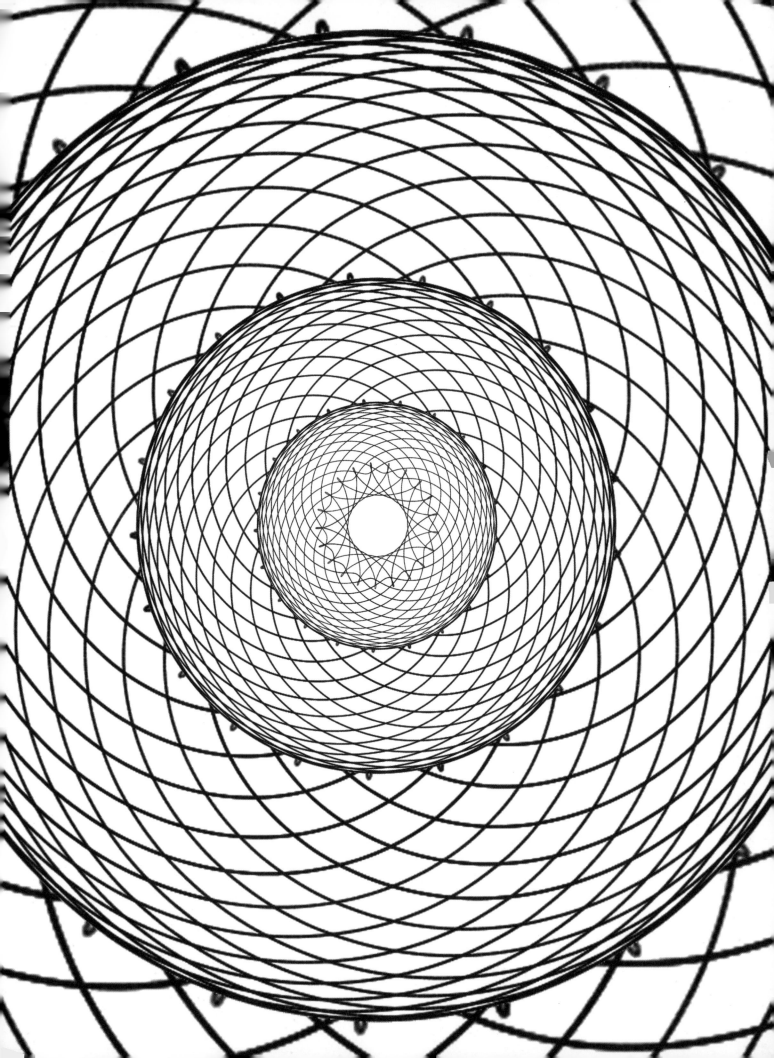

"**Mindfulness is about love and loving life. When you cultivate this love, it gives you clarity and compassion for life, and your actions happen in accordance with that.**"

Jon Kabat-Zinn

"Our own worst enemy cannot harm us as much as our unwise thoughts. No one can help us as much as our own compassionate thoughts."

Buddha

"Life is available only in the present moment. If you abandon the present moment, you cannot live the moments of your daily life deeply."

Thích Nhất Hạnh

"In today's rush we all think too much—seek too much—want too much—and forget about the joy of just being."

Eckhart Tolle

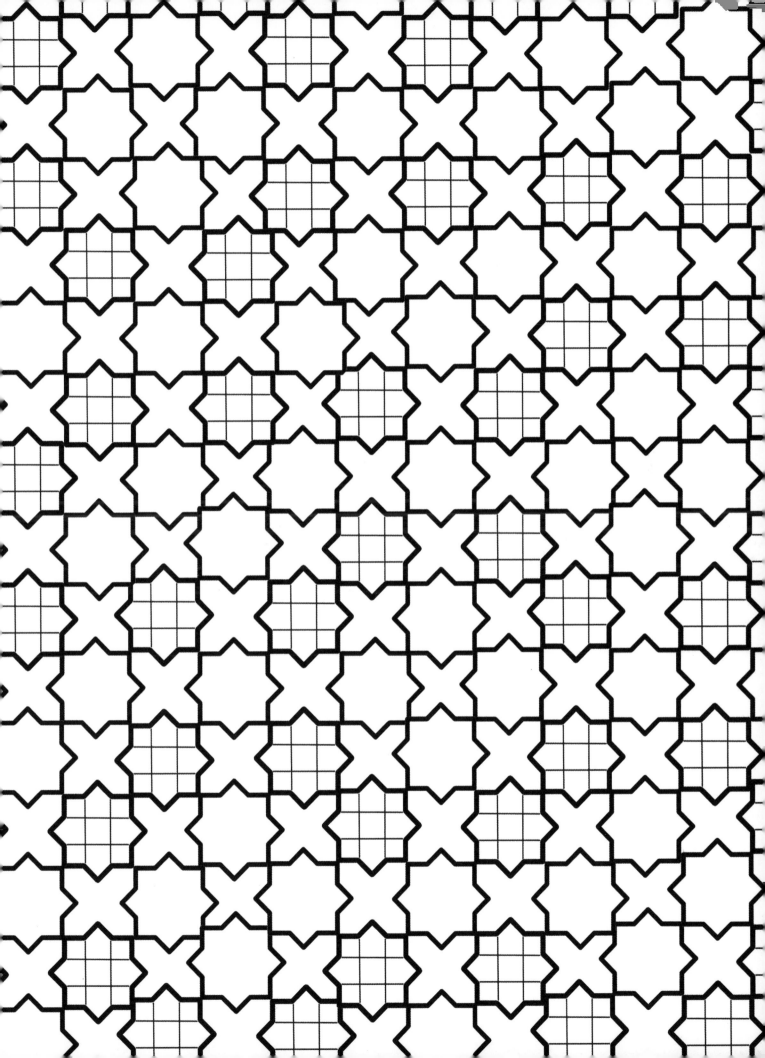

"Nothing brings down walls as surely as acceptance."

Deepak Chopra

"There is a vitality, a life force, an energy, a quickening that is translated through you into action, and because there is only one of you in all time, this expression is unique."

Martha Graham

"We must let go of the life we have planned, so as to accept the one that is waiting for us."

Joseph Campbell

"Life is a preparation for the future; and the best preparation for the future is to live as if there were none."

Albert Einstein

"If you clean the floor with love, you have given the world an invisible painting."

Osho

"In the end, just three things matter: How well we have lived. How well we have loved. How well we have learned to let go."

Jack Kornfield

"If a man is called to be a street sweeper, he should sweep streets even as Michelangelo painted, or Beethoven composed music, or Shakespeare wrote poetry. He should sweep streets so well that all the hosts of heaven and earth will pause to say, 'Here lived a great street sweeper who did his job well'."

Martin Luther King, Jr.

**"Today is the first day
of the rest of your life."**

American proverb

"There is nothing either good or bad, but thinking makes it so."

William Shakespeare

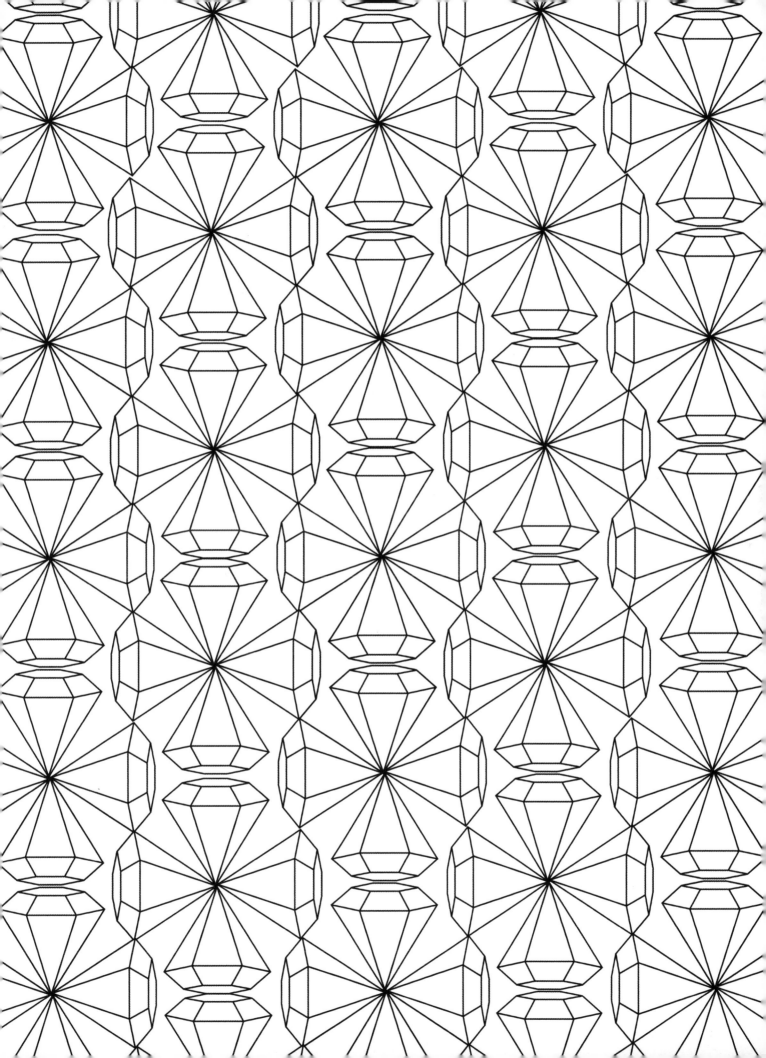

"Go confidently in the direction of your dreams! Live the life you've imagined. As you simplify your life, the laws of the universe will be simpler."

Henry David Thoreau